Hummingbird Soul Haven

Luna Lotus

BookLeaf Publishing
India | USA | UK

Made with ❤ on the BookLeaf Publishing Platform
www.bookleafpub.in

Dedication

This book is dedicated to the souls who have lost their voice. May you find it again

Acknowledgement

A special thanks to the poets who have come before me and the ones who will come after me. This endeavor would not have been possible without the encouragement of my family and friends. I would like to express deep appreciation to all those who have inspired me to pursue this passion.

Preface

It has been a dream to have my poetry come to life in the pages of a book. I am so grateful for the opportunity to share this collection with those special souls who have supported me in my journey of self-discovery. My hope is that all who read the poems will be inspired and be reminded of the light that is always within. May you never stop chasing your dreams.

My New Ego

My new ego is taking over me
A psychological change
is necessary
Your life is a gift
Why must you not want to live
The very air that you breathe
is the essence of me
Unalome transformation
A one day reprieve
I kept coming back
Overwhelming became falling together
instead of falling apart
My diamond heart
shines bright

Floating

I don't want the ocean to leave me
I swam all day
moving from here to there
without a care
this is my home with Poseidon I roam
to the depths of the ocean
I have known the peace of the water around
me
I want to see the sun one more day to splash
and play
where seagulls call
floating clouds that just don't care

Essence of Creation

the sound of the rain
the orchestra of mother nature the swirling
chills of a breeze covers me in bliss
the gentle sway of the willow tree
the howl of the wolf
my trusted guide
its time to rest
the night sky embraces me in a glorious vision
the moon appears
whispering to me
love is near love is near
peace rains down like petals on a rose
mother nature
the essence of creation
weaving golden threads
that binds us together
united as one

Soul Music

strumming the strings of soul music
the light of the moon
illuminating the magic of the night
the crisp air
wrapping me in a cacoon
a million stories told to me in the stars
the lights dancing above me
a new found strength fluttering around me
quietly whispering
take a breath
dance to the music of your soul

Flourish

the hummingbird whispered to me
flourish child
the red rocks surrounding me
sycamore trees standing tall hugging me
cool water rushing over me
restoring the scattered pieces of me
adventure thrills me
green vibrant alive
reaching my hands to the sky
sunshine rains down on me
flourish child
you have eagle vision
soar above to the blue sky
allowing the storms to pass you by
luminous warrior
sing your battle cry
flourish child

The Green Hummingbird

The green hummingbird is so majestic
she sings a love song all day long to me
It's in the scones and in my bones
you have given me a home away from home
Free to roam
pastures of gold
visions of turquoise horses grazing in the
breeze
the cowbell rings
the green hummingbird sings
time to spread your wings again
The heart of art is calling
tears are falling
creating a river of promise
the green hummingbird sings
It's always dark before the dawn
You no longer need to carry the sorrows of
yesterday
The tide has turned
the green hummingbird sings
windchimes sway in the willow trees

Your barn your rules
Lemonade wishes turn to horse kisses
The green hummingbird is so majestic

Diamonds Shine

Diamonds shine
blinding my eyes
dancing in the kitchen
You are forgiven
Don't live in regret
the endless thoughts swirling around
softened by a morning prayer
Diamonds shine
write it down
lift your hands to the sky
what a gift to be alive
awaken to the voices of nature
breathe in the limitless energy
believe in your light
diamonds shine
visionary

Awakening

My eyes open yet I am still asleep
I listen quietly to the birds chirping
singing to me their song of praise
inhale exhale breathe peace
move swiftly they repeat
embrace a retreat
create a space to shine your light
my body longs for the embrace of my golden
armor
rise from the trauma, triggers and power
struggles
flow like the gentle breeze you feel on your
skin
images unfurling in my mind's eye
traveling swiftly through different worlds
the bluebird's story slowly unfolds
keys floating in stories told
awakening wisdom that is centuries old
quietly freedom chimes ring
can you hear the awakening

Cinnamon Embers

Cinnamon Embers
light the flame
a new beginning is unfolding
layers upon layers
stories told to you by your fathers
lies
darling you are the star
in a dark haze rage circles
swallowing you into a painful memory
of who you used to be
she is not there anymore
angels sing the song of cinnamon embers
keep your gaze forward
flutter gracefully
ever so slowly to a place
that is safe and carries you to a new place
keep track of the spears
they are intended to ignite your fears
darling you are the star
light the flame
only cinnamon remains

Who is She

Stained glass windows
shining all around me
I can feel your spirit
flowing through me
the sun the moon the stars
reminding me
mosaics of endless eternity
surrounding me
seeking grace that cradles me
in moments of anxiety
the sound of your breath
reminds me of a love never known
so far from home
whispers of synchronicities
the bluebird singing to me quietly
reminding me the time to shine
has come to pass
the past is a painting
the poetry is you
raindrops washing into an endless rainbow
of a new you
take the leap
jump into the sea of peace

the bridge to eternity leading me
golden fields of light greeting me
thankyou beautiful soul
for the music to inspire me
there is a masterpiece staring back at me
who is she
she is me

Birdsong

We had only just begun
this love song
has started out all wrong
turn up the volume they
are playing my song
the one of redemption and karma
all along
The birds sing their song all day long
without a care in the world
they face the elements
with limitless grace
suspended in time
a reminder of the sublime
no matter what the color or the weather
birds of a feather
always flock together
turn up the volume
birdsong

Lipstick Queen

Lipstick Queen
she yells fix your face
the lipstick queen
walks tall with grace
not a worry on her face
the lipstick queen knows
the magic of color, glitter and shimmer
why must I cry for the sound of silence
shaking shuttering stuttering
please no more violence
find your balance
pick any color
they are all beautiful
fix your face she yells
your smile will transport
you to another love
the color of unconditional love
lipstick queen

You Deserve A Throne

You deserve a throne
the sorrow
the lies
the words that cut deep and easy like a knife
You deserve a throne
the rage that keeps
you awake at night
twisted tormented
by the fear that has been fed
to you since you were a child
You deserve a throne
wall whispering screams
whirlpools of wicked manipulation
You deserve a throne
rivers of tears
flowing for years
souls calling for grace
black clouds erased
you deserve a throne
white roses
shower you in a sweet embrace
you deserve a throne

We Stand Tall

We will stand tall
let the skyfall
bold vivid golden
moments together
your breath becomes mine
colors collide
limitless moments in time
the clouds turn
from black to white
violet flames dancing
in my mind
what was broken
now melting into
metallic colors
blinding light
the vicious cycle collapsed
surrounded by a turquoise
dream turned
gold at last

Windfall Faith

Windfall faith
will take you
to a land
where you can stand tall
windfall faith
the chains
of pain lifted
by amazing grace
diamonds in the sky
firefly eyes
surrender to the quiet
rhythm of rest
windfall faith
a bridge to serenity
love is my guiding light
leading me to
hummingbird haven
manifest destiny

Shine

May the light
of a thousand suns
shine down on you
May your weary heart
find peace
a garden of possibilities
growing in your mind
together mending
the scars of the dark
watercolor dreams
ignite the spark
imagine dreams
become reality
one step at a time
living in perfect
harmony
a sanctuary of positivity
shine

Ocean Flower

ocean flowers
Islands of isolation
calls of desperation
sunset galleries
beautiful catastrophe
chimes of reality
rain down
what shall be shall be
said the wise old owl in the tree
on a wing of devotion
arrows cross oceans
flowers of emotion
calculated evolution
intuition is my crown
unapologetically soul courage
engulfs me
ocean flowers
sage hours
a web of gold and grace
ocean flowers

Create

create
crystal towers
celestial hours
walk with me
take my hand
discover a paradise
blue roses appear
sunkissed serenity
hummingbirds fluttering in the air
wind-chimes swing in the air
playing sweet melodies of hope
the waves of the ocean
washing away despair
love is in the air
be still and float to paradise
dance on the seashells
create

Limitless Path of Existence

the day I drank the moon
blissful restoration
comforts my soul
moonbeams dance
for all of cosmic time
diamonds passing
through the hourglass
of blessings
falling like snowflakes
not one the same
each with its own
unique design
weaving the web of
divine connection
like the heron standing in stillness
we must continue our souls
adventure but remain steadfast
trust in that perfect moment
like the heron we will move with grace
The sun will shine upon the kind
and provide clarity of mind body and spirit

Trust the splendid adventure that awaits
create love in all of your endeavors
It is there you will soar with
courage peace and serenity
May each day be colorful
rest in gratitude
miracles happen

Reprieve

Message in a bottle
the smell of saltwater fills the air
A slight chill in the morning air
the coolness greeting me so gently
pouring a cup of gratitude coffee
my body slowing stirring
sighs of relief for the day
that welcomes me
sitting up to catch
the first glimpse of light
a sky tapestry of gold
appears in the distance
my eyes dance with delight
a masterpiece of reprieve is before me
a smile for miles
soul reprieve
this canvas of colors
rays of reprieve

Listen Unconditionally

listen unconditionally
sounds of chaos
hands trembling
tears falling
listen unconditionally
sounds of joy
hands clapping
tears falling
listen unconditionally
sounds of silence
hands open
tears falling
listen unconditionally
sounds of love
hands caressing
tears falling
listen unconditionally
sounds of peace
doves fly
listen unconditionally
what a gift
listen unconditionally